Grandpa.
Christmas 2009

Love Brie & Brendan

FRONT COVER: CA. 1922 • Miss Jim draws a crowd at the St. Louis Zoo. Miss Jim was purchased six years earlier through a fund-raising campaign sponsored by the Zoo and the city's newspapers.

PREVIOUS PAGE: 1957 • Tim and Janie Thomas, Christie and Pattie Kelly have fun with the suds that suddenly appeared at the waterfall in Forest Park. Park officials suspect a prankster deposited detergent in the pool.

2004 • The St. Louis Symphony Orchestra celebrates its 125th year with a performance on Art Hill, overlooking the Grand Basin.

ST. LOUIS POST-DISPATCH

THE JEWEL OF ST. LOUIS
FOREST PARK

BY SALLY J. ALTMAN AND RICHARD H. WEISS

THE JEWEL OF ST. LOUIS
FOREST PARK

BY SALLY J. ALTMAN AND
RICHARD H. WEISS

DESIGNER: Kelly Ludwig, Ludwig Design
COPY EDITOR: Laszlo Domjan
SALES AND MARKETING: Gail LaFata
PRODUCTION ASSISTANCE: Jo Ann Groves
Special thanks to Doug Weaver of *Kansas City Star* Books

First edition, first printing
ISBN: 0-9796054-1-3
Printed in the United States of America by
Walsworth Publishing Co., Marceline, MO

To order additional copies, call 1-800-329-0224
Order online at www.post-dispatchstore.com

Special thanks to J. Stephen Bolhafner, the recently retired news
researcher at the *Post-Dispatch*, and Duane Sneddeker, curator
of photographs and prints for the Missouri Historical Society, who
provided invaluable assistance and advice. Though this book reflects
on the park's history, it is not by any means comprehensive. For that
we recommend *Forest Park* by Caroline Loughlin and Catherine
Anderson, published in 1986 by the Junior League of St. Louis and
University of Missouri Press. We relied on it and the *Post-Dispatch*
archives for many of the facts contained herein.
— Sally J. Altman and Richard H. Weiss
October 2007

1943 • Fans surround Miss Jim, who at this point was 65 years old and ailing. Over the years thousands of children had enjoyed rides on her broad back.

2004 • A view of the renovated Grand Basin and the Art Museum, at the rise of Art Hill.

THE STATUES OF FOREST PARK

1 **Apotheosis of St. Louis**
Charles Niehaus, 1903
Dating from the World's Fair, this sculpture of the city's namesake was the city's official symbol until Eero Saarinen's Gateway Arch.

2 **Jewish Tercentenary Memorial**
Carl Mose
A monument celebrating the 300th anniversary of the founding of the first Jewish settlement in the U.S.

3 **Edward Bates Statue**
J. Wilson McDonald, 1876
The first statue erected in the park (although at a different site), it commemorates a local lawyer who was Lincoln's attorney general.

4 **Friedrich Jahn Memorial**
Robert Cauer, 1913
On the site of the World's Fair German Pavilion, this memorial commemorates the "father of gymnastics."

5 **Frank Blair Statue**
Wellington W. Gardner, 1885
A U.S. senator, Blair seized the U.S. Arsenal during the Civil War, keeping the city and much of the state from joining the rebellion.

FOREST · PARK

MISSOURI HISTORY MUSEUM

VISITOR CENTER & PLAYGROUND

Grand Dr.
CRICKET FIELD

Deer Lake

Theatre

Lagoon Dr.

NORMAN K. PROBSTEIN GOLF COURSES

3

8

Grand Basin

DWIGHT DAVIS TENNIS CENTER

BOATHOUSE

1

THE MUNY

Skinker Blvd.

ST. LOUIS ART MUSEUM

Post-Dispatch Lake

Summit Dr.

Union Dr.

4

WORLD'S FAIR PAVILION

PRAIRIE

Government Dr.

KENNEDY FOREST

Washington Dr.

Concourse Dr.

ST. LOUIS ZOO

JEWEL BOX

9

Wells Dr.

10

Hampton Ave.

64 40

TURTLE PARK

Oakland Ave.

·········· Wheels path   ------- Heels path

Fact text by Joe Holleman | Post-Dispatch, and Sally J. Altman; Statue text by David Bonetti | Post-Dispatch   SOURCES: "Forest Park" (1986, Junior League of St. Louis and University of Missouri Press), by Caroline Loughlin and Catherine Anderson; Missouri Historical Society

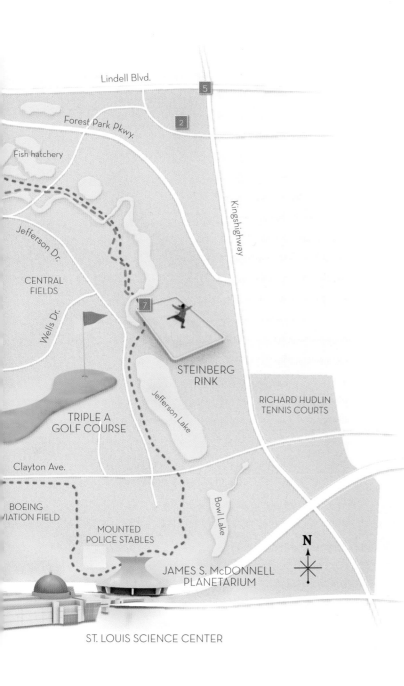

Fish hatchery

Lindell Blvd.

Forest Park Pkwy.

Jefferson Dr.

CENTRAL
FIELDS

Wells Dr.

Kingshighway

STEINBERG
RINK

Jefferson Lake

TRIPLE A
GOLF COURSE

RICHARD HUDLIN
TENNIS COURTS

Clayton Ave.

Bowl Lake

BOEING
AVIATION FIELD

MOUNTED
POLICE STABLES

JAMES S. McDONNELL
PLANETARIUM

N

ST. LOUIS SCIENCE CENTER

Illustration by Rich Rokicki | Post-Dispatch

6 Franz Sigel Statue
Robert Cauer, 1906
The German-born Sigel
organized a regiment of
German-American volunteers
to fight for the Union.

7 Joie de Vivre
Jacques Lipchitz, 1962
One of the only modernist
sculptures in the park,
by a prominent member
of the School of Paris.

8 Placebo
Roxy Paine, 2004
A work of contemporary
conceptual art that makes
itself at home in the park.

9 St. Francis of Assisi Statue
Carl Mose, 1962
Another nondescript statue
by the man responsible
for the Stan Musial statue
at Busch Stadium.

10 Animals Always
Albert Paley, 2006
Officially part of the Zoo, this
100-ton weathering-steel sculpture
is intended to raise consciousness
of endangered species.

CONTENTS

10 INTRODUCTION:
Memories By The Million

16 THE VISITOR CENTER:
A Very Good Place To Start

22 THE ART MUSEUM:
Worth The Climb

42 MISSOURI HISTORY MUSEUM:
First And First Class

50 SPORTS:
Any And Every Game You Could Imagine

68 THE MUNY:
Drama Writ Large

84 PEOPLE IN THE PARK:
Meander At Will

110 SCIENCE:
The Total Package, Including The Ribbon

120 WORLD'S FAIR:
Meet Me In Forest Park

140 AROUND THE PARK:
The Magnificent Restoration

156 EVENTS IN THE PARK:
Much Ado About Something

168 THE ZOO:
The Crowd Pleaser

3

2000 • Alice Bloch and Frank K. Flinn welcome the first sunrise of the new millennium on Art Hill.

4

1923 • Even though it's hibernation time — February — members of the Washington Glee and Mandolin clubs have a rapt audience in the bears at the St. Louis Zoo.

1976 • Jude Howard finds a friendly perch for studying.

<<< 1941 • Even in January, a sunny day brings visitors to the park. The Chase and Park Plaza buildings can be seen in the background.

1904 • The battle of Santiago de Cuba Bay, during the Spanish-American War, was re-enacted twice a day during the 1904 World's Fair. The men are "wearing" the ships to control their movement.

INTRODUCTION: MEMORIES BY THE MILLION

More than 2.8 million people live in and around St. Louis. We are different in so many ways, but what we all share is Forest Park.

We met at the waterfall, married at the Jewel Box, danced the night away at the World's Fair Pavilion.

We laughed at the antics of Siegfried the walrus, paid homage to Phil the gorilla and smashed our snouts into slushy sno-cones at the Zoo.

We saw Lindy fly over and Ethel Merman bring down the house.

We arrived in buggies, streetcars, Model Ts and Humvees. We waltzed in starched collars and ermine stoles and rocked out in flip-flops and halter tops.

We baked. We froze. We got soaked. We fell out of a tree, skinned our knees and cursed as we one-hopped our Titleists into the River des Peres.

We lucky folk got in free at the zoo and nearly everywhere else on most days and for many things.

If you are among the fortunate who have visited this jewel of St. Louis even once, then you will revel in the pages that follow. You'll visit the park's buildings, stroll along its pathways and stop at scenic vistas

In the beginning, of course, you would have found simply a forest. So thick was the foliage that residents referred to the western edge of the park as "the wilderness." The River des Peres meandered through on a southeasterly course with sport fish

jumping along its way. The park was a 40-minute carriage ride — and a far cry — from downtown St. Louis. There residents were packed into row houses and shanties, many breathing air fouled with soot.

Forest Park was a dream shared by a handful of visionaries, most persistent among them the real estate developer Hiram Leffingwell. It was not an easy sell. Too much land was involved at too much cost ($600 an acre!). And while they paid higher taxes, opponents feared land speculators would get rich.

But over a decade's time, plans were formulated and reformulated, objections were met and overcome. By the opening June 24, 1876, Maximillian G. Kern, the superintendent of the park and a landscape gardener, had seen to the construction of 19 miles of road for scenic carriage rides, 20 miles of walking paths, a Hippodrome racetrack, numerous kiosks and a bandstand surrounded by a manmade lake and accessible only by bridges.

Nearly 50,000 people gathered on a characteristically steamy afternoon to open "the people's park." By then St. Louis, with a population surpassing 300,000, was the fourth largest city in the United States, host to the Democratic National Convention and now it could boast of a playground half again larger than New York's Central Park.

"I present to you … this large and beautiful Forest Park for the enjoyment of yourselves, your children and your children's children forever," declared Chauncy F. Shultz presiding justice of the St. Louis County Court. "The rich and poor, the merchant and mechanic, the professional man and the day laborer, each with his family and lunch basket can come here and enjoy his own … all without stint or hindrance … and there will be no notice put up, 'Keep Off the Grass.'"

1927 · More than 100,000 people gather on Art Hill to cheer the return of Charles A. Lindbergh after his nonstop trans-Atlantic flight in the Spirit of St. Louis.

11

2001 · The bronze statue of King Louis IX by moonlight. The Louisiana Purchase Exposition Company, managers of the 1904 World's Fair, presented this statue of the patron saint of St. Louis in 1906.

>>> **CA. 1932** · This photograph would have made a nice holiday card. A view of Art Hill from the Grand Basin.

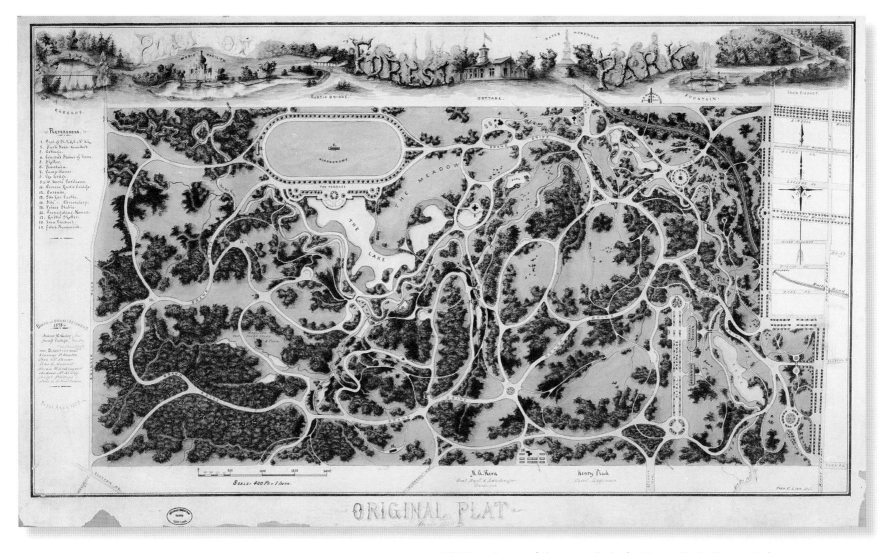

1875 • A map of the original plat for Forest Park. The park's first superintendent, Maximillian G. Kern, told his supervisors that no money could be found for some features in the plan, such as the Cascades. But he included them to drive public interest.

1875 • Grading begins in Forest Park. The work provided jobs for 300 .

THE VISITOR CENTER:
A VERY GOOD PLACE TO START

A visit to the park should start at the Visitor Center. Or it could end there. It could even be a stop-off in the middle of your day. Just don't miss it. It's the first visitor center the park has ever had. But the building itself — or at least a portion of it — has been in the park since 1892.

Just as its earliest advocates hoped, from its opening, the park filled with people. In its earliest years, most visitors arrived by horse and carriage or by train. They came to cool off under the trees, boat on the lakes, watch a horserace at the Hippodrome or picnic with family and friends. Still, the remoteness of the park created a barrier for many until the city established a streetcar line in 1885 with a 5-cent fare.

With tens of thousands of people riding streetcars on weekend visits to the park, city and park officials were eager to provide a shelter from the heat, rain and snow. In 1892, they opened the Lindell Pavilion, its crowning feature an imposing clock tower.

With the growth of athletics in the park, the building was remodeled for use as a locker room for tennis and golf in 1914. A fire in 1925 razed the pavilion, leaving only a portion of its clock tower standing.

In 1927, the Field House was constructed on the foundation of the Lindell Pavilion. Like its predecessor, the Field House housed locker rooms and a pro shop. It also included a restaurant and refreshment stand serving visitors throughout the park.

The old streetcar pavilion went through another metamorphosis in 2003. After extensive renovation, including restoration of the original structure's clock tower, the Field House was reopened as the Dennis and Judith Jones Visitor and Education Center. The Visitor Center offers walking tours of the park, multi-generational educational programming, a Teacher Academy, a café, banquet and meeting rooms — and locker rooms.

2003 • Martin Hernandez and Alberto Luis clear the front walk of the Dennis and Judith Jones Visitor and Education Center, the latest incarnation of the Lindell Pavilion.

>>> 1920s • The Lindell Pavilion, a streetcar shelter at the park's north-central entrance, opened in 1892. It was remodeled for use as a locker room in 1914. Fire destroyed the building in 1925.

1997 • A view of the Visitor Center clock tower. Time had stopped for more than two decades until contributions from local residents brought about a restoration.

<<< **1940** • Soft drinks and snacks are served to visitors to the Field House.

20

1949 • The Field House (now the site of the Visitor Center) is decimated by fire. The center now provides information for tourists, and serves as as a locker facility for golfers, tennis and handball players as well as a 19th hole.

2006 • A runner warms up in the recently-renovated Dennis and Judith Jones Visitor Center before heading out on the running path.

THE ART MUSEUM:
WORTH THE CLIMB

t's hard to imagine Forest Park without the St. Louis Art Museum. The imposing limestone and brick beaux-arts-style building designed by Cass Gilbert, is the only remaining structure in the park from the 1904 World's Fair besides the Zoo's bird cage. It's framed by two statues, symbolizing sculpture and painting, on either side of its front steps. And then there's the statue of King Louis IX of France, bedecked in armor and sword, and mounted on his steed. Before the building of the Gateway Arch in the 1960s, the statue was recognized as our city's icon. (The sword itself has been a magnet – for thieves and vandals. It has been replaced many times.)

1977 • Snow envelopes the statute called "Sculpture," outside the entrance to the Art Museum.

1956 • The R.H. Russell family of Clark, Mo., visits a portrait of themselves that was included in the Family of Man photographic exhibition at the St. Louis Art Museum.

King Louis overlooks Art Hill and the beautiful Grand Basin, a focal point of the World's Fair and of St. Louis for the more than a century.

If there's a single informal gathering spot and playground for St. Louisans, it's Art Hill, a Mecca for sledders in the winter and picnickers in the summer. In 1918, John Philip Sousa conducted a band concert on Art Hill before 200,000 people to raise money to support the war effort. Nine years later, more than 100,000 people turned out to welcome Charles Lindbergh after his trans-Atlantic crossing.

The city's Art Museum opened in downtown St. Louis in 1881 and came to the park two decades later, a decision met with mixed emotions. It took a long uphill trudge to the museum without a buggy or car.

Throughout its history, the Art Museum has encouraged the public to enjoy its resources through special educational programming for children and adults and with special exhibitions. In 1940, about 47,000 people attended an exhibition of the works of Picasso. More than 260,000 people visited the museum in 1976 to view Monet's Years at Giverny. And in 2005, approximately 100,000 turned out for Treasures from the Royal Tombs of Ur.

Today the museum boasts a per capita attendance that is among the highest of art museums in the country. In 2006 nearly half a million visitors managed to make their way up the hill.

1919 • Visitors to the park walk between the Grand Basin and a waterway created for the World's Fair.

1945 • The people watching is always as interesting as the art work.

>>> **2001** • The Art Museum in a show of patriotism following the terrorist attacks on 9/11.

1947 • Taking a break from sledding, a crowd warms up by a log fire at the top of Art Hill.

<<< 1939 • It's a long, steep walk back up Art Hill, and even some of the most enthusiastic sledders need some help to the top.

1940 • Staff from the Art Museum unpack Picasso paintings for an exhibition. Forty thousand people came to the museum for the show.

1937 • Art Hill asks sledders to pay a price.

1985 · A balloon launch from the Art Museum's International Children's Art Festival provides a stunning backdrop for the statue of King Louis IX.

<<< 2006 • The Grand Basin and the Art Museum sparkle in the evening lights.

1987 • Relishing the opportunity to enjoy the museum without crowds while attending an evening fundraiser, Michele and Thomas Costello consider "Keith" by Chuck Close.

<<< 1984 • It's a lot tougher to hang something on the outside of the museum than inside. These workmen are preparing to rappel down the front of the museum after installing bolts for an exhibition banner.

1960 • It takes concentration to create a masterpiece, and this young man is well on his way.

2006 · It doesn't get much better than fresh snow on Christmas morning. Joe Daus takes his daughter, Jessica, for a ride.

>>> **1951** · The snow is deep and the hill is getting icy, but Ray Smith is heading down Art Hill for "just one more" run to the basin.

1977 • Clements L. Robertson examines his work on renovations to the paintings in this gallery.

40

MISSOURI HISTORY MUSEUM:
FIRST AND FIRST CLASS

Little known fact: Forest Park is home to the first Jefferson Memorial. At the conclusion of the 1904 World's Fair celebrating the centennial of the Louisiana Purchase, organizers were eager to create a lasting memorial to the man who closed the deal. Built with proceeds from the Fair, and a like contribution from the city of St. Louis, the Jefferson Memorial opened its doors in 1913. Twenty-five years later, the folks in Washington, D.C., got around to building their own.

Our Jefferson Memorial is located at what had been the main entrance to the Fair, on the north side of the park at DeBaliviere Boulevard. The centerpiece of the building is a 16-ton marble statue of Thomas Jefferson, created by Karl Bitter, the chief sculptor for the World's Fair. Jefferson is posed seated, gazing out at visitors as they approach the park.

The Jefferson Memorial was built to house the city's collection of World's Fair memorabilia and documents and artifacts related to the Louisiana Purchase. It was also meant to provide a home for the Missouri Historical Society, an organization formed in 1866 and dedicated to "saving from oblivion the early history of the city and state..." The society put itself on the national map in 1927 when it put on display the Lindbergh collection of more than a thousand medals, scrolls and gifts. The collection drew 1.5 million visitors in the first year alone.

To be candid, the Missouri History Museum grew a bit stale in later years. A visit there in the '70s and '80s could be underwhelming when compared to the Zoo or Art Museum. But the History Museum got a $4 million financial boost in 1987 when voters in St. Louis city and county allowed it to join the Zoo-Museum taxing district. With sustained support from the district and major gifts, the History Museum was able to triple in size in 2000 with the opening of the Emerson Center. The facility includes an auditorium and space for large traveling exhibitions, classrooms and a restaurant. The History Museum drew national acclaim in 2004 for its role in the Lewis & Clark National Bicentennial Exhibition. It now features a permanent state-of-the art exhibit of the history of St. Louis.

1999 · A Juneteenth celebration at the Missouri History Museum features music by the Bosman Twins.

>>> **1934** · Students from Central School in Ferguson start their tour of the Jefferson Memorial with a look at the third president.

2005 • While waiting for the start of the groundbreaking ceremony, Elizabeth "Libby" Schueddig holds a time capsule to be buried in the new playground near the Jefferson Memorial. The playground, also adjacent to the Visitor's Center, is designed for children with and without disabilities.

>>> **1972** • An underground addition to the Jefferson Memorial includes galleries, a library, an auditorium and storage space.

1915 • A view down DeBaliviere Avenue after an August flood.

<<< 1932 • The Charles Lindbergh exhibit drew huge crowds to the Jefferson Memorial.

1959 • The River Room exhibit at the Jefferson Memorial spurs a youngster's imagination.

>>> **2006** • The Jefferson Memorial with its fountains makes a grand entrance for the park.

SPORTS:
ANY AND EVERY GAME YOU COULD IMAGINE

They started early, these games. They ended late. And when that wasn't enough, they put in gas lamps and electric lights. They played golf, tennis, handball, soccer, croquet, rugby, lacrosse, lawn tennis and ultimate Frisbee, for goodness' sakes.

People came to play as early as 4:30 a.m. on Forest Park's first tennis courts, built in 1912. In 1917, gaslights were added, allowing play to be extended to 9:30 at night. Golfers, always the hardiest and addicted of breeds, would play through the winter.

One man stands out as the father of amateur athletics in the park. He was Dwight F. Davis, park commissioner from 1911-1915 and the Davis in the vaunted Davis Cup tennis tournament. The primary purpose of a park, Davis once said, "is the raising of men and women rather than grass and trees." And so acres of land were cleared for playing fields, courts and courses. Nine holes of golf were opened in the summer of 1912 and available seven days a week. Within a year it grew to 18, and then another nine-hole course was added. For more than a decade St. Louisans could play on them for free.

Under Davis and his successors, hosts of leagues and teams were created. A national bike race was held in the park in 1925. The first Silver Skates Carnival followed a year later in the Grand Basin.

The park filled with people playing their games — just as its creators had imagined. But not all people. Until 1923, African-Americans were told they would have to wait to play golf until a separate course was built for them. Then the door opened, but just a crack. African-Americans could tee off but just on Mondays, from 6 a.m. until noon. Racial segregation extended to the tennis courts and other facilities as well. It wasn't until the late 1940s that court rulings ended separate and unequal in the park.

2002 • Robert Mifflin sends his electric model airplane soaring at Forest Park.

>>> 1909 • Pilot Glenn H. Curtiss in flight over Forest Park during an aero competition. Aviation Field at the south end of the park opened in 1920 for mail flights between St. Louis and Chicago. The trip took three and a half hours.

1992 · The clubhouse at the Dwight Davis Tennis Center. It's open to the public and has the amenities of a private club.

>>> **2000** · Beginners and world champions have graced the courts in Forest Park. Five-year-old Selina Wilkinson knows it's not all about hitting the ball over the net; you have to retrieve those balls, too.

2002 • The Triple A Golf and Tennis Club opened in the park in 1897. Steve Wald and his son, Robert, are scoping out their next shot.

>>> **1943** • Doris Peterson and R.E. Whitesell take advantage of a mild February day to play a round of golf.

2003 · Chester Coleman (right) tees off with his friend Ray Rush at the Norman K. Probstein Golf Course.

>>> **1929 ·** The second tee at the Forest Park Golf Course offers a challenge and a spectacular view.

<<< **1933** • Bee Bechestobill, Bee Slater, Alice Carnoske and Nina LaRue practice in Forest Park for the North American Indoor Skating Championships.

2001 • It's tough to keep your feet under you on the first day of the season. Autumn Nieters, 4, struggles to stay upright at Steinberg Rink. The rink got a $1.4 million facelift in 2001.

1985 • Jennifer Martin, 2, isn't convinced that her spin around the rink with her dad, Tom, will be all that much fun.

⟩⟩⟩ 1957 • After seeing skaters on the ice rink in Central Park during a visit to New York, Etta A. Steinberg decided a rink would be a wonderful addition to Forest Park. Steinberg Rink opened in 1957, delighting 234,740 skaters in its opening year.

1927 · A good game will always draw a crowd in the park.

2003 • A brief rain, followed by a beautiful rainbow, doesn't stop the game in the park between De Soto High School and St. Louis University High School.

>>> **1919** • Dwight Davis and his successors as park commissioner encouraged the use of the park for organized athletics of all sorts, including polo.

65

1999 • The handball and racquetball courts at Forest Park are used year-around.

>>> **1898** • By the 1890s, color on her checks and perspiration (not sweat) on her brow are signs of a healthy, active woman. Lawn tennis, boating, horseback, sledding and skating are all popular activities.

THE MUNY:
DRAMA WRIT LARGE

In the summer of 1914, the Pageant Drama Association produced a city-wide theatrical production called the Pageant and Masque of St. Louis. It featured a cast of thousands – about 7,000 to be more precise — presenting a history of the 150-year-old city in which love triumphed over war and poverty. Such a large cast guaranteed a good showing of friends and relatives, but when 100,000 assembled on Art Hill, the people who ran the park knew they were on to something big — very big.

The Pageant Drama Association followed its success with another production in 1916, the performance of *As You Like It* in honor of the 300th anniversary of the death of Shakespeare. There was another huge cast — 1,000 performers from St. Louis and around the country — and the audience was equally as impressive. The production took place in an open-air amphitheater, framed by two oak trees east of Art Hill.

Twice encouraged, civic leaders and business pooled their resources and built a permanent 10,000-seat, outdoor theater at the site. The St. Louis Advertising Club produced *Aida* on the site in June of 1917. The *St. Louis Post-Dispatch*, in reviewing the opening night performance, lauded the sightlines and acoustics, but complained about the vagaries of the weather (the performance was rained out after the second act).

And it was ever thus. Huge audiences, a grand stage and quirky weather. In 1919, the drama enthusiasts created the Municipal Theater Association of St. Louis, and planned six weeks of musical theater for the summer. The Muny was launched.

The Muny is the largest outdoor theater in the country. It has been the site of patriotic gatherings, fashion shows, Easter sunrise services and a memorial service one year after the death of President John F. Kennedy. Generations of St. Louisans have been entertained there with song, dance and story. It has inspired actors and playwrights. It has dazzled children and captivated adults. To many St. Louisans, summer begins when the Muny opens its doors. The smart ones bring a fan and an umbrella.

1981 · The Nathan Frank Bandstand is the second bandstand on Pagoda Island. You can admire this one from afar, but you can't walk to it. It can only be reached by boat.

>>> 2003 · When the house is full, Muny performers play to an audience of 10,779 fans. It's the largest outdoor theater in the U.S.

1916 • The production of *As You Like It* marking the 300th anniversary of Shakespeare's death. It was held on the site of what is now The Muny.

<<< 1883 • The Music Pagoda, built in 1876, charmed visitors in the early years of Forest Park. But it was closed in 1911 because of structural safety concerns and destroyed by fire a year later.

1916 • One of the actors in Shakespeare's *As You Like It*. She was among a thousand players from St. Louis and around the country. The productions over a week-long run drew an average of 8,000 a night.

>>> **1973** • Debbie Reynolds and George S. Irving in a revival of Irene, a musical comedy originally produced in 1919.

1939 • A chorus line practices steps in preparation for another outdoor season

1947 • Janet Dunphy can hardly believe that she might not be a perfect fit for The Muny chorus. Her sister, Judy, listens as dance director Dan M. Eckley works with Janet.

>>> 1946 • The girls line up for last-minute makeup flourishes.

2007 · Muny volunteers Natalie Bram and Elliot Burton encourage audience members to dance with them while waiting for *Hello Dolly!* to begin.

1974 • In some families, Muny seats are passed from generation to generation. When individual tickets go on sale, crowds line up early at the box office — and bring their chairs with them for the long wait.

1944 • Hat in place, Gloria Sicking, a chorus member in *The Open Road*, carefully pulls on the rest of her costume for a dress rehearsal.

<<< 1946 • As children wait to be called for tryouts, their families and friends press against the fence surrounding the rehearsal stage, hoping for good news.

1941 • It can be a long wait between calls to the stage. Betty Herbert and Rosemary Powell fill the down time with knitting.

>>> **1960** • Ralph Blane, musical composer for *Meet Me in St. Louis*, gathers members of the chorus around the piano for a rehearsal.

PEOPLE IN THE PARK:
MEANDER AT WILL

Please walk on the grass. Run, bicycle, walk your dog, fish, sail your boat and play in the water. From its earliest days, Forest Park was intended as a retreat from the work-a-day world, a refuge from the city heat, an escape to a play land. Its roads were designed to meander through the woods, and if you got lost, so be it. Park officials resisted installing directional signs well into the 1940s.

In 1879, park officials began stocking lakes with fish. In the 1930s, fly and bait casting contests were a national event, drawing many spectators to watch participants break national and world records. But it wasn't until 1945 that fishing was allowed in the park lakes. And initially, only children could fish. The limitations were gradually eased, and by 1972, they were removed completely.

In early 1894, the *St. Louis Post-Dispatch* conducted a fund-raising campaign to cover the cost of extending the length of the park's largest lake, Peninsular Lake, to approximately three-quarters of a mile. Boaters filled the lake in summer; skaters circled its surface in winter. Park workers scoured the ice with wire brushes to allow smooth skating and torches were put up around its edges so skaters could enjoy themselves into the evening.

1940 • With a mix of sun and shade, hills and straight-aways, the jogging path through the park is always compelling for runners.

>>> 1937 • A long cool drink and then off to play again. Dogs are regular park-goers, too. They join their owners on the walking path, at the Boathouse for a meal and even in the boats.

From its earliest days, there has been tension over who had the right of way on Forest Park's paths. Carriage drivers complained about bicyclists. Everyone on foot worried about the horses, buggies and cyclists. In 1898, a cinder bicycle path was built and a bicycle parade celebrated its completion. Separate paths were created for equestrians, bicyclists and visitors who walked the promenades. Later it was roller bladers and joggers, weaving among the dog walkers, who caused headaches and collisions. With the recent restoration of the park, hard and soft trails have created a path to peaceful co-existence for those on wheels and those on heels.

1978 • The Cascades, a 75-foot waterfall on the hill west of the Art Museum, is named after stair-stepped fountains at the World's Fair. It's the perfect playground on a hot summer day.

<<< **1890** • Sketch class in the park.

CA. 1903 • Whether it's by carriage or on foot, a Sunday tour of the park, decked out in weekend finery, is a must.

1924 • It's the same view, the Lindell entrance to the park, but 20 years later on an Easter Sunday the carriages are replaced by a parade of automobiles.

1898 • Weekends and picnics in the park are a long St. Louis tradition. Over the years the dress may change, but not the site.

1992 • Nearly 200 members of the Brooks family get together for good food and good times.

1880 • Trees came down in the western portion of Forest Park to make way for the World's Fair grounds. This pretty drive through the birches disappeared with the Fair.

1955 • Damaged trees and limbs are free to the public when cleared from the park.

1940 • The park is a retreat from the oppressive summer heat in St. Louis. Beginning in 1911, city officials lifted the evening curfew during heat waves, and people slept on sheets and blankets that they chilled in their iceboxes during the day.

1920 • As an alternative to nights in a hot hotel, in 1919 the Automobile Club of St. Louis set up "tourist camps" on the southern border of the park where travelers could sleep in tents and hammocks. The camp was removed in 1925

2002 • Kevin Allen juggles fishing gear and his three sons, Kendell, Kameron and K. Carlton, as they celebrate Father's Day in the park.

>>> 1942 • State and national competitions for fly and bait casting were held in Forest Park beginning in the 1930s. Meets were open to an enthusiastic public.

SWIMMING
OR WADING
ALLOWED.

1968 · Swimmers find the rocks in the pond by the Planetarium to be a great launching pad.

<<< 1971 · It's 90 degrees and the day calls for cooling off in the water — no matter what the sign says (or doesn't say).

1951 • James Lodes and George Hubbell set to sail their boats on a warm spring day.

>>> CA 1907-08 • Fish have been raised in Forest Park since the 1880s. But until 1945, no fishing was allowed in the park. Employees of the Missouri Fish Commission seined fish from the park lakes and transferred them to other lakes in the state.

2007 • Amy Kreher and Kenny Alonzo spend a quiet — but hot — afternoon in the park.

>>> **1991** • Joggers run over the river and through the woods.

1963 • Terry, Deborah and Anita Blake think these drinking fountains are "just right."

1941 • Forest Park provided a haven for hundreds of soldiers on leave from Fort Leonard Wood. The tent city was located at the southeast end of the park near Kingshighway and Oakland Avenue.

1998 • Charlie and Julie McIntosh hitch a ride with their mom, Beth.

<<< 2003 • Some 18,000 trees grow in Forest Park. The most heavily wooded area is the Kennedy Forest. In recent years, savanna and grasslands have been restored in the park, enhancing its natural beauty.

2001 • A father and daughter take to the park path for a little exercise and fresh air.

2005 • Separate paths around the park lessen the risk of a mishap between wheels and heels

SCIENCE:
THE TOTAL PACKAGE —INCLUDING THE RIBBON

On February 20, 1962, John Glenn became the first American to orbit the Earth. The United States was engaged in an international space race with the Soviet Union — and the Soviets appeared to be winning. Americans everywhere were intent on coming from behind. The people of St. Louis, home of McDonnell Aircraft, a company with a huge stake in the space program, were no exception. As everyone looked to the skies, the McDonnell Planetarium opened in Forest Park in April 1963.

Spurred by the widespread interest in the space race, visitors flocked to the Planetarium. Within four months, 100,000 people had walked through its doors. (No telling how many left with their heads stuck at a 45-degree angle.) Three thousand visitors came the day a full-scale model of the Apollo space capsule was put on display.

In 1970, a prank began a tradition at the Planetarium. Local students wrapped the Planetarium in a red ribbon for the Christmas holiday — and what began as a joke was continued as a hallmark of the holidays with local businesses donating the funds and the ribbons.

In 1983, the Museum of Science and Natural History acquired the Planetarium and closed it for renovation. It reopened two years later as the St. Louis Science Center. In 1991, the Science Center built a second facility on Oakland Avenue with a pedestrian bridge spanning the highway and connecting it to the Planetarium. In its first two months, the St. Louis Science Center became the most visited science museum in the world. The Exploradome was added in 1997 to house special exhibits. With more than 700 exhibits, the Science Center is an ever-changing wonderland of exploration -- and one of only two science centers in the country with free general admission.

2001 • More than 9,000 stars are projected in the dome of the McDonnell Planetarium. It opened in 1963 at a time when interest in space was high as the United States raced the Soviet Union to the moon.

>>>1965 • Rex and Trudy Nicolay peer into a full-size model of the Apollo space craft on display at the Planetarium.

2005 • Steven Huber, a Science Center employee, tests a Segway scooter, a new form of transportation for tours of Forest Park.

2006 · The projector at the Omnimax Theater in the St. Louis Science Center sends images onto a domed screen. With its large-format film and enhanced sound system, audience members find themselves the middle of the movie action.

1982 • Repairs to the Planetarium roof are a challenge to workers. The structure is a hyperboloid, a shape described by a mathematical equation

1977 • Workers wrap the Planetarium in a holiday bow. This annual tradition began as a prank in 1970.

2005 · Visitors walk through the tunnel from the Science Center to the Planetarium.

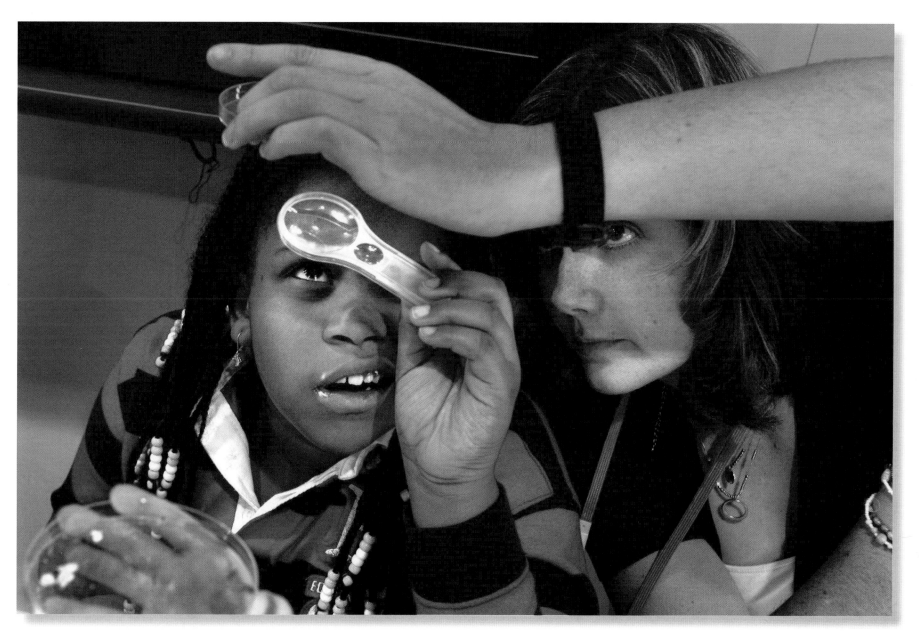

2006 • A mobile science teaching lab from the Science Center travels to local schools. Jada Gipson, from Spoede Elementary School, looks at mealworms with the help of her teacher, Darci Cadieux.

2006 · Juli Donahue experiences gravitational pull on a G-force ride at the Science Center.

2000 • Jack Raney peers through the window in the floor of the crosswalk spanning Highway 40 between the Science Center and the Planetarium.

WORLD'S FAIR:
MEET ME AT FOREST PARK

In 1901, the St. Louis Municipal Assembly passed a bill providing park land for a World's Fair. An amendment excluded Forest Park. Many thought the St. Louis World's Fair, officially titled the Louisiana Purchase Exposition, should be in Carondelet Park or O'Fallon Park, both of which bordered the Mississippi River. The river, after all, had played such an important role in the Louisiana Purchase. They feared the Fair would destroy the park's natural assets with construction and traffic. Besides, if people came to Forest Park for the Fair, where else would they visit in St. Louis?

But Forest Park was centrally located and by then thoroughfares had been established that made it the most accessible of the sites. So new legislation was passed and on the day after the park's 25th anniversary, June 25, 1901, city officials announced the World's Fair would be held in Forest Park in 1903. Actually it took a year longer.

Nearly half of Forest Park was devoted to the Fair: 657 acres on its western boundary, the acreage known as "the wilderness." Trees were burned and stumps were uprooted with dynamite as the wilderness was cleared for the Fair's buildings and pathways. Pavilion Lake was drained and reshaped. As part of their agreement, Fair organizers pledged to return the park to its original condition within a year. It would, in fact, take nearly a decade.

Distinguished architects from across the U.S. designed the Fair buildings based on a ground plan conceived by Cass Gilbert of New York and Frank Howe of Kansas City. Their vision called for palaces of mixed Greek and Roman architecture, fanned out on the top of what's now known as Art Hill. The buildings for the Fair were made of a temporary material, a mixture of plaster of Paris and fiber, called staff. But this temporary construction wasn't adequate for the Palace of Fine Arts, the building displaying valuable art work from around the world. It had to be fireproof. A permanent building of limestone and brick was constructed for the Palace of Fine Arts — the future home of the St. Louis Art Museum.

Nearly 20 million people visited from April 30 to Dec. 1, 1904. Let's join them for a look.

1904 • Ceylonese dancers, along with entertainers from other exotic locales, perform on The Pike.

>>> 1904 • The Ferris Wheel came to St. Louis from the 1893 Chicago World's Fair. People are lifted 250 feet into the air in cars that hold 40 passengers each. A ride on the wheel costs 50 cents.

1904 • Debate has raged for years on whether or not the ice cream cone was invented at the 1904 World's Fair. Regardless, it's fair to say that our Fair certainly popularized the cone, as well as hot dogs and iced tea.

>>> 1904 • The Fair is a celebration of science and progress. But The Pike is a street for fun. The saying "what's coming down the pike" originated at the Fair. Visitors to the mile-long Pike would go to a Wild West show, watch dancing girls, ride a roller coaster or buy souvenirs.

1904 • A German village is recreated along The Pike. The German Tyrolean Alps housed a restaurant where a banquet was held for President Theodore Roosevelt during his November visit to the Fair.

1904 • The Palace of Electricity is an imposing sight when lit at night. Most homes didn't have electricity at the time of the Fair. Visitors saw the latest in electrical applications including X-ray machines and wireless telephones.

1904 • A network of canals cross the fairgrounds. This is a view from the Grand Basin, looking west. The Ferris Wheel can be seen in the distance.

Filipino soldiers

1904 · Filipino army scouts parade and drill on the Fair grounds.

<<< **1904** · The Graceful Fountain tops The Cascades, a series of fountains with waters flowing down Art Hill into the Grand Basin.

JOHN E. MURPHY,
U. S. Secret Service.   THOS. H. CARTER.   THE PRESIDENT AND MRS. ROOSEVELT.   PRESIDENT FRANCIS.   WM. LOEB.   WILLIAM DESMOND,
Chief of Detectives.

L. D. DOZIER.   MRS. ANDREWS.   MRS. MONTGOMERY.
MRS. MANNING.   W. H. THOMPSON.
MRS. FRANCIS.

PRESIDENT ROOSEVELT IN REVIEWING STAND ON PRESIDENT'S DAY, NOVEMBER 27TH.

2004 · Tyrone and Gerrick Fortenberry play with flashlights during the 100th anniversary celebration of the World's Fair in Forest Park.

<<< **1904 ·** President Theodore Roosevelt (third from the left) and his wife, Edith, (sitting next to him) visit the World's Fair. Among the dignitaries he meets with is David R. Francis, president of the Louisiana Purchase Exposition Company (next to Mrs. Roosevelt).

2004 • The Giant Wheel is brought to Forest Park to celebrate the 100th anniversary of the World's Fair. A maintenance employee greases the wheel's axle.

>>> **1943** • At the end of the Fair, workers demolished the Ferris Wheel and buried it on park grounds. William Jones, who worked for the wrecking company, shows a piece of the wheel uncovered by park employees during a dig for the wheel remnants.

1904 • Festival Hall is the centerpiece of the Fair. Thousands of lights outline the building and are used in a nightly light show. The building houses a 3,500-seat auditorium and the world's largest pipe organ. (After the Fair, the organ is moved to Wanamaker's department store in Philadelphia.) In front of the building is The Cascades fountain. The Palace of Fine Arts building (part of the St. Louis Art Museum) is just visible behind Festival Hall to the right.

>>> **1904** • A group of orphaned children gather at the Belgium Pavilion before a day at the Fair.

1904 • A view toward the west, with Festival Hall on the near left, the Palace of Electricity on the near right and the Palace of Machinery in the center background. The Palace of Machinery houses the enormous generator for the Fair and the pumps for The Cascades waterfall.

>>> 1904 • The first Olympic games in the U.S. are held at the St. Louis World's Fair. Field events are held at Washington University's Francis Field. Here, swimmers wait for the start of a race held on the Forest Park fairgrounds.

1904 · Below the Grand Basin is the Plaza of St. Louis. It is where official Fair ceremonies are held. A monument to the Louisiana Purchase was at one end of the Plaza and the original statue of King Louis IX of France reigned over the other end.

AROUND THE PARK:
THE MAGNIFICENT RESTORATION

Formal landscaping, an imposing stairway, cherry trees and a lighted fountain grace the hill below the World's Fair Pavilion. Over the years it has been used for special events of all kinds, joyful and mournful. Among the most festive: the Forest Park Forever hat luncheon. It celebrates generations of St. Louisans who created and helped restore the park.

St. Louisans may complain that their civic leaders have let them down. But no one says that about the people of Forest Park Forever. The nonprofit organization was founded in 1986 to work with the city on the shared goal of making Forest Park one of the finest urban parks in the country. Since then, consistent with a master plan approved in 1995, more than $94 million in private and public funding has been raised and invested in the restoration of the park.

The work included the grand refurbishing of the pavilion -- which by the way was built after the Fair as part of the restoration of the park. Park Commissioner Dwight Davis had once proposed glassing-in the pavilion for use as a conservatory. That never happened, but the park got its floral conservatory in 1936 with construction of the Jewel Box. Its unusual cantilevered 50-foot glass walls and metal horizontal structure maximized light and minimized hail damage.

From its opening, the Jewel Box drew St. Louisans like bees to honeysuckle. Each year, hundreds of thousands of visitors came to enjoy the seasonal floral displays. By the mid-1970s, attendance had declined and park funds were pinched. Forest Park Forever came to the rescue in 2002, spurring a $3.5 million renovation that renewed the Jewel Box's luster.

The Boathouse is another of FPF's major successes. From its opening, St. Louisans have been drawn to the lakes and ponds and lagoons at the park. They could find rental facilities and launch sites at many of the lakes, but none was particularly elegant. In the summer of 2003, a new boathouse was added to the shores of Post-Dispatch Lake, with a year-round restaurant. The lake was expanded once again, and boaters can now travel more easily to the Grand Basin, into lagoons and around islands dedicated to wildlife and picnicking.

1992 • Boating is a favorite activity in the park. Canoeists on Post-Dispatch Lake enjoy a summer day.

>>> **1897** • Women, as well as men, take their turn at the oars on a Forest Park lake. Thousands of people lined the lake shores in the 1890s to watch competitive rowing events.

FOREST PARK.
E.Boehl.Phot.

1923 · The World's Fair Pavilion at the top of Government Hill is graced with formal gardens and a regal staircase.

2003 · Since its recent renovation, the Jewel Box shines as a wedding venue.

>>> **1953** · The Jewel Box is a popular spot for wedding photographs.

2004 · Greg Lamprecht and Molly Jones take their drinks and conversation to a paddleboat parked at the Boathouse on Post-Dispatch Lake. The restaurant welcomes diners -- and their well-behaved dogs.

>>> **1930** · Sailing model boats as big as three feet long and more than seven feet tall is such a popular pastime that it causes traffic jams when passing drivers slow down to watch.

1968 • There isn't much breeze and the days aren't warm yet but that doesn't keep the sailors off the Grand Basin in early March.

2005 • The Jewel Box is the first floral conservatory in the park but it's not the first building with that name. In 1916, a gardener in the park created floral displays in one of the greenhouses that drew wide acclaim. That greenhouse became known as a jewel box. When this conservatory was built in 1936, park officials appropriated the Jewel Box name.

>>> **1941** • Elaborate seasonal floral displays charmed Jewel Box visitors. This Easter display includes more than 5,000 lilies in addition to an assortment of other flowers.

1954 • On a June day with a high of 95 degrees, a ride in a motor boat through the park lagoons is just the ticket.

2007 • Sarge, the dog, skippers the paddle boat crewed by Jeff Grace and Mark Jaffe as the three compete in the annual Paddle With Your Pooch Dog and Master Boat Race sponsored by the Boathouse in Forest Park.

<<< **1938** • Lucky Day campers line up for a canoe race.

EVENTS IN THE PARK:
MUCH ADO ABOUT SOMETHING

Like many cities, St. Louis is divided by race, by class and by neighborhood. But Forest Park is a mixmaster where nearly everyone blends easily nearly all the time. Our park accommodates a crowd quite nicely -- from opening day in 1876, when 50,000 people showed up for the park's dedication, to 1906 when 25,000 people gathered in front of the Art Museum for the unveiling of the statue of St. Louis, to the more than 100,000 people who gathered at Art Hill in June 1927 to welcome Charles A. Lindbergh back to St. Louis after his nonstop flight from St. Louis to Paris.

In 1907, more than 100,000 people gathered at the Aero Grounds on Newstead Avenue, near Forest Park, to watch nine balloons take off in an international hot air balloon race. A century later, a similar number attended the Great Forest Park Balloon Race. By 2007 the race was a 35-year tradition in Forest Park, and among the highest attended single-day sporting events in the country.

No way to know for sure, but certainly Forest Park is among the most popular walk-a-thon, ride-a-thon spots in the Midwest, if not the country.

It is a place where people pray and march for justice. When civil rights leaders here memorialized Martin Luther King after his assassination in 1968, they began their march downtown and ended it at the park.

2001 • Roderick Hill, as Benvolio, and Charles Boland, as Tybalt, rehearse for a performance of *Romeo and Juliet*. The Shakespeare Festival of St. Louis produces a play that runs for several weeks each summer in the amphitheater just east of the Art Museum.

>>> 2005 • Liftoff for the annual Great Forest Park Balloon Race.

Forest Park is a hothouse for experimentation and new ideas that grow and take root as enduring traditions in our civic life. Perhaps the best and most recent example is the Shakespeare Festival of St. Louis, which opened with *Romeo and Juliet* on June 2, 2001. On an unusually cool night, many in the audience of 3,000 arrived more than two hours before curtain to picnic, listen to strolling musicians and watch dancers on the Forest Park slopes before they tucked themselves into blankets and sleeping bags for the play. More than 32,000 attended the free productions that first year: in 2007, a record 53,800 turned out for *Much Ado About Nothing*.

2006 • Bring your lawn chairs and blankets, a picnic dinner and the kids. The Shakespeare Festival of St. Louis is an evening of pure pleasure.

Frank Starke, Photo.

St. Louis, Mo.

Second Annual St. Louis County Tour.

L. A. W.

1999 • Up, up and away at the Great St. Louis Kite Festival in Forest Park.

<<< **1892** • Members of the League of American Wheelmen gather by the Frank Blair statue near the Lindell entrance to the park before the second annual St. Louis County Bicycle Tour.

2003 · Mary Keirle and her daughter Neale Rebman honor the ice cream cone and memories of the 1904 World's Fair at the annual Forest Park Forever hat luncheon.

>>> **2003** · Yolanda Cazer is elegantly bedecked for the annual Forest Park Forever hat luncheon at the World's Fair Pavilion.

2003 • Thomas Thale entertains revelers at a New Year's celebration at the Zoo.

<<< 2007 • The Humane Society of Missouri's annual Bark in the Park fundraiser brings pugs Frank and Lucy to the park with sisters Mia, Sarah and Gloria Maciorowski.

2004 • Pilots illuminate the park at the balloon glow on the hill below the World's Fair Pavilion.

2006 • Cindy Tower builds a sculpture of aluminum cans and plastic soda bottles at the St. Louis Earth Day festival.

THE ZOO:
THE CROWD PLEASER

The world-renowned St. Louis Zoo, now populated with 3,600 animals in state-of-the-art breeding, research facilities and habitats, started with a collection of deer, geese and prairie dogs in a handful of cages.

A zoo was not first on Maximillian G. Kern's to-do list when he took over as the park's first superintendent. But he did pitch the idea to include a modest zoological collection that would be free as "an institution of public instruction and amusement."

By 1895, park department employees got the Zoo up and running. They soon added a herd of buffalo, elk and Clint the dromedary. Enclosures for the animals were built with private donations.

The modest collection grew rapidly at the close of the World's Fair. Animals that had been on display at the Fair were donated — or simply left — at the Zoo. By 1916, residents were so enamored that they approved a tax to support the Zoo's animals and property. As part of the campaign for the tax, the Zoo, with the support of the local newspapers, sponsored a penny drive among St. Louis school children to raise money for a new elephant. It was enough to buy Miss Jim, who arrived in April of that year.

The '20s and '30s saw the addition of the bear pits, primate house, reptile house and bird house. Phil the gorilla and two giant pandas, Happy and Pao Pei, were brought to the Zoo in the 1930s.

Visitors loved the giraffes, the zebras and the seals. They could even ride Miss Jim.   But nothing pleased St. Louisans like the animal shows, begun in the 1930s.

These acts are no longer considered appropriate at zoos, which now emphasize education and preservation over entertainment. Beginning in 1970 with the end of the "big cat" show, the St. Louis Zoo phased out most of the performances. The chimp show ended in 1982 and the elephants took their final bows in 1992. Visitors can still catch a sea lion show and some smaller events in the Children's Zoo.

The Zoo draws 3 million visitors a year, by far the most popular attraction in the park. Miss Jim and Phil would be proud.

1979 • A new born chimp grabs a strand of Carol Fieseler's hair. Fieseler, an assistant supervisor at the Zoo, was showing off the chimps, the first born at the Zoo in 11 years.

>>> **1978** • It doesn't look too comfy but this Kodiak bear finds the rocks to be the perfect pillow on a warm day.

CA. 1906 • The early animal cages in the park are a far cry from the naturalistic habitats created in later years.

1922 • Two young women record their visit to the Zoo with a photograph on an elephant.

1998 · Charles Hoessle, (right) director of the St. Louis Zoo at the time, and Harold Chance on one of the miniature trains that visitors can ride through the Zoo.

>>> **1949** · Willy the monkey wanders the Primate House making friends with Susan Brant and her cousins, Vivian and David Nulsen.

1934 • The giant bird cage was built for the federal government exhibit at the 1904 World's Fair. Visitors walked through a tunnel in the cage, with nearly 1,000 birds flying overhead.

>>> **1918** • The seals always attract a crowd with their playful antics and agility on the rocks and in the water.

1934 • Toto Tembo, a baby elephant, is unloaded from a plane at St. Louis Field en route to his new home at the Zoo.

>>> **1934** • Toto Tembo with Terengosi, an African keeper who accompanied the baby elephant to the Zoo and stayed for a few weeks.

<<< 1962 • Jules Jacot leads the tigers through their routine in the Lion Arena.

1976 • Siegfried, a 3,000-pound walrus, is a crowd-pleaser, regularly entertaining Zoo visitors while playing with a floating log in his pool outside the Aquatic House.

1962 • Robbie Spencer beams with pleasure as he hugs a young goat at the Nursery Village in the Zoo.

<<< **1960** • Two sisters ride a Galapagos tortoise at the Nursery Village in the Zoo. Only the arms and legs of one sister are visible as she holds on tightly in the hopes of staying on the ride.

1952 • Roy and Pancho, decked out in new sneakers, join Irene Mowrey for a walk at the Zoo.

<<< 1957 • It's hard to say who is watching whom. Phil the gorilla keeps a watchful eye on the visitors to his cage. Phil is 525 pounds, and not yet fully grown.

2006 · *Animals Always*, created by sculptor Albert Paley, is made of 100 tons of steel (that's the weight of 20 elephants) and includes more than 60 animals among trees, ferns and other plants. It's located at the Hampton Avenue entrance to the Zoo.

>>> 1935 · Giraffes arrive at Forest Park after a long trip by boat, rail and truck from East Africa.

1922 • The city bought the bird cage at the Zoo from the federal government at the end of the World's Fair.

<<< 1961 • The Cards are on their way to a fifth place finish in the eight-team National League, but maybe help is on the way.

PHOTO CREDITS

ST. LOUIS POST-DISPATCH STAFF PHOTOGRAPHERS

Michael J. Baldridge: 98

Paul Berg: 97

Katherine Bish: 164

Andrew C. Bruening: 85

David Carson: 1, 38, 44, 65, 112

Robert Cohen: 4, 21, 109, 117, 118, 132

Sarah Conard: 102

Wayne Crosslin: 115

Andrew Cutraro: 66

Ted Dargan: 40-41, 114

Bill Dyviniak: 39

Dan Eldridge: 78

Karen Elshout: 34, 49, 52, 54, 60, 91, 103, 107, 162, 163, 184

Renyold Ferguson: 99, 180

Wendi Fitzgerald: 12

J.B. Forbes: 22, 27, 87, 110, 188

Jack Gould: 182

Jack January: 82

Sam Leone: 96, 155, 157, 169

Lester Linck: 79

Erik M. Lunsford: 53

Cynthia Metcalfe: 108

Huy Richard Mach: 146, 165

Dawn Majors: 16, 106, 167

Kevin Manning: ii-iii, 131, 166

James McKenzie: 113

Jerry Naunheim Jr.: 36, 116, 156, 161

Wes Paz: 35

Aaron Pennock: 56

Teak Phillips: 59, 69

James A. Rackwitz: 19, 148-149, 179

Dave Regier: 168

Laurie Skrivan: 119

Victor Stevenson: 18, 84

Gabriel Tait: 50

Risdon Tillery: 32

Larry Williams: 33, 140

Arthur Witman: 81

Staff file photos: iv, 5, 6, 20, 23, 24-25, 26, 28, 30-31, 37, 43, 45, 55, 58, 61, 62-63, 64, 68, 74-75, 76, 77, 80, 83, 88, 89, 93, 94, 100, 104, 111, 133, 142-143, 145, 151, 152-153, 154, 171, 173, 174, 176, 177, 178, 183, 185, 186, back cover

MISSOURI HISTORICAL SOCIETY ARCHIVES:

Emil Boehl: i, 15, 17, 67, 141

O.C. Conkling: Cover, 175, 187

John H. Gundlach: 71, 72

George F. Heffernan: 57

Keepstone View Co.: 128

Theodore Link: 14

Ed Meyer: 29

W.C. Persons: 13, 147

Paul Piaget: 48

Frederick Pitzman: 47

Ralph A. Rugh: 10-11

George Stark: 92

Frank Starke: 160

William H. Trefts: 51

Unknown: 8-9, 42, 46, 68, 70, 86, 90, 101, 105, 120, 121, 122, 123 124-125, 126, 127, 129, 130, 134, 135, 136, 137, 138-139, 170

OTHER PHOTOGRAPHERS

Forest Park Forever: 150

Joseph Abeles/Sy Friedman: 73

George S. Pietzcker: 95

Shakespeare Festival of St. Louis: 158-159

Susan Jackson: 144

Bill Greenblatt: 172

UPI: 7, 181

1998 • The Living World has an ever-changing variety of interactive exhibits demonstrating the interdependence of animals, plants and people in our world. The sphere in the front of the photo is a small self-sustaining ecosystem, called "A Little Earth."